Your Guide to Government

What is the legislative branch?

James Bow

Crabtree Publishing Company

www.crabtreebooks.com

Crabtree Publishing Company

www.crabtreebooks.com

Author: James Bow
Coordinating editor: Kathy Middleton
Series editor: Valerie J. Weber
Editors: Valerie J. Weber, Lynn Peppas, Crystal Sikkens
Proofreaders: Sangeeta Gupta, Kelly McNiven
Discussion questions: Reagan Miller
Production coordinator: Ken Wright
Prepress technician: Ken Wright
Project manager: Summit Kumar (Q2A Bill Smith)
Art direction: Joita Das (Q2A Bill Smith)
Cover design: Samara Parent
Design: Roshan (Q2A Bill Smith)
Photo research: Ranjana Batra (Q2A Bill Smith)
Print coordinator: Katherine Berti

Written, developed, and produced by Q2A Bill Smith

Photographs:
Cover: Shutterstock; Title page: Shutterstock; P4: Gary718/Shutterstock; P5: United States Government Work; P6: Architect of the Capitol; P7: Sara D. Davis/Getty Images News/Getty Images; P8: Chip Somodevilla/Getty Images News/Getty Images; P9: Scott J. Ferrell/CQ-Roll Call Group/Congressional Quarterly/Getty Images; P10: Linda Davidson/ The Washington Post/Getty Images; P11: Harris & Ewing(tl); P11: Superstock/Glow Images(bl); P11: Alex Wong/Getty Images News /Getty Images(br); P12: Alex Wong/Getty Images News /Getty Images; P13: Chip Somodevilla/Getty Images News /Getty Images; P14: Chip Somodevilla/Getty Image News/Getty Images; P15: Andrew Harrer/Bloomberg/Getty Images; P16: Scott J. Ferrell/CQ-Roll Call Group/Congressional Quarterly/Getty Images; P17: Mark Wilson/Getty Images News/Getty Images; P18: Brendan Hoffman/Getty Images News/Getty Images; P19: Tom Williams/CQ-Roll Call Group/ Roll Call/Getty Images; P20: Joshua Roberts/Bloomberg/Getty Images; P21: Mark Wilson/Getty Images News/Getty Images; P22: Sarah L. Voisin/ The Washington Post/Getty Images; P23: Bill Clark/CQ Roll Call Group/Roll Call/Getty Images; P24: Andrew Harrer/Bloomberg/Getty Images; P25: Ryan Kelly/Congressional Quarterly/Getty Images; P26: Alex Wong/Getty Images News /Getty Images; P27: Ullstein bild ullstein - ullstein bild/Glow Images; P28: Mario Tama/Getty Images; P29: Everett_Glow/Glow Images; P30: AFP/Getty Images; P31: Scott Olson/Getty Images News /Getty Images.

Library and Archives Canada Cataloguing in Publication

CIP available at Library and Archives Canada

Library of Congress Cataloging-in-Publication Data

CIP available at Library of Congress

Crabtree Publishing Company

www.crabtreebooks.com   1-800-387-7650

Printed in Canada/022013/BF20130114

Published in Canada
Crabtree Publishing
616 Welland Ave.
St. Catharines, ON
L2M 5V6

Published in the United States
Crabtree Publishing
PMB 59051
350 Fifth Avenue, 59th Floor
New York, New York 10118

Published in the United Kingdom
Crabtree Publishing
Maritime House
Basin Road North, Hove
BN41 1WR

Published in Australia
Crabtree Publishing
3 Charles Street
Coburg North
VIC 3058

Contents

The Three Branches

In the United States, the government makes the laws. It decides what taxes you pay and how much money your school gets. It also chooses whether our country goes to war during times of conflict. It is a big job. Many people work in the government.

Most people know who the president is. They know less about who works with the president to run the country.

The U.S. government is split into three parts. The president and the people who work for the president form the executive branch. They make the laws work. The judges of the Supreme Court are part of the judicial branch. They decide what the laws mean.

President Barack Obama is our 44th president.

4

The legislative branch meets in the Capitol in Washington, D.C.

The legislative branch of the government is called **Congress**. It makes the laws. Lawmakers decide what rules or laws would help the country. They put their ideas about helpful rules in bills. Lawmakers talk about these bills and then they vote on whether the bills should become law.

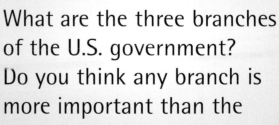

WHAT DO YOU THINK?

What are the three branches of the U.S. government? Do you think any branch is more important than the others? Why?

5

The Legislative Branch

Congress is made up of 535 lawmakers. Each lawmaker has a seat, or place, in Congress. The House of **Representatives** and the Senate make up Congress. They suggest the laws and vote on them.

The House of Representatives is not a real house. Instead, the House describes the group that works together to make the laws. The House and the Senate both meet in the Capitol in Washington, D.C.

The Rotunda is a large, round room in the center of the Capitol.

Most people vote on election day. Others vote earlier. Together they decide who gets to go to Congress.

But who are these people? Why are they there? The United States is a democracy. Therefore, representatives of the House and the senators of the Senate are elected to office by voters on election day.

In a democracy, the people decide what the government should do. But we do not have time to make all the decisions. So we choose lawmakers to act for us. This process is called representative democracy.

House of Representatives

With 435 lawmakers, the House of Representatives is the biggest part of Congress. Each representative is from a **district** somewhere in the United States. About 700,000 people live in each district. Sometimes the district is part of a city, but sometimes it is a whole state! No matter where you live, someone represents you in the House.

Members of the House are known as congressmen or congresswomen. They are elected to serve for two years. Then they have to be elected again. They meet, talk, and vote to make or change the laws that govern the United States.

Members do this by introducing bills. Before a bill becomes a law, it has to be passed by the House and the Senate. Then the president must sign it.

Representatives meet in the House Chamber to make laws and vote on them.

Voting on bills is the most important job of Congress. But the House has some powers that the Senate does not have. For example, only the House can introduce bills that raise taxes.

The bills that representatives vote on can be huge.

Speaker of the House

The House of Representatives picks the Speaker of the House. The Speaker is usually the leader of the **political party** that has the most seats in the House. The Speaker of the House is the most powerful position in Congress.

The Speaker is in charge of the House. He or she **presides** over meetings or sessions. The Speaker "sets the agenda." This means that they decide which bills will be debated and voted on.

In many ways, the Speaker shapes the laws of the country more than the president. In 2010, John Boehner became Speaker of the House.

Nancy Pelosi was the first female Speaker of the House.

The Speaker can schedule his or her party's bills to make sure they get the most attention. This is partly what makes the Speaker's job such a powerful one.

The Speaker follows the vice president in the line of command. Imagine that the president dies or cannot do his or her job. Then the vice president takes over the position. If the vice president cannot carry out the job, then the Speaker would become president.

WHAT DO YOU THINK?

Why is the Speaker of the House so powerful?

11

The Senate

The Senate is the smaller part of Congress. Just 100 lawmakers work in the Senate.

Every state sends two senators to Washington, D.C. Senators serve six-year terms. Every two years, one-third of the Senate's seats are up for election. Senate elections are **staggered**. A state never votes for both of its senators at the same time.

The Senate's main job is the same as the House's. Senators talk about and vote on bills that might become new laws.

Like the House, the Senate has its own special duties. For example, the president chooses people to help run the government. These people include judges on the Supreme Court and other courts. The Senate must approve of these people.

The Senate meets in the Senate Chamber in the Capitol. Senators say the Pledge of Allegiance at the beginning of each meeting.

WHAT DO YOU THINK?

How long can a senator be part of the Senate?

Three people were elected president while they were still senators: William Harding, John F. Kennedy, and Barack Obama.

13

President Pro Tempore

The vice president is in charge of the Senate. When the vice president is away, senators pick their own leader. This leader is called the *president pro tempore*. *Pro tempore* means "for now." The president pro tempore is like the Speaker of the House but is not as powerful.

Sometimes the Senate vote for a bill is tied. Then the vice president makes the deciding vote. The president pro tempore cannot break a tie, however. If the vice president is away, the bill is defeated, meaning it is no longer up for consideration and is officially dead.

Patrick Leahy became the president pro tempore of the Senate on December 17, 2012.

The president pro tempore is not as powerful a position as the Speaker of the House, but it is respected. He or she follows after the vice president and the Speaker in the line of command to be president.

Robert Byrd was a senator from 1959 to 2010. He became the president pro tempore in 1989. Byrd was the longest-serving senator in the U.S. Congress.

Majority and Minority

Who is in charge of the House and the Senate? It depends on which political party holds the most seats. It sounds like a game of musical chairs. But it is serious business.

A political party is a group of people who share the same ideas about how to run the country. There have been many parties in U.S. history.

Right now, power is split between the Republicans and the Democrats. Most senators and representatives belong to one party or the other.

The party with the most members in the House or the Senate is the **majority** party. The other party is the **minority** party.

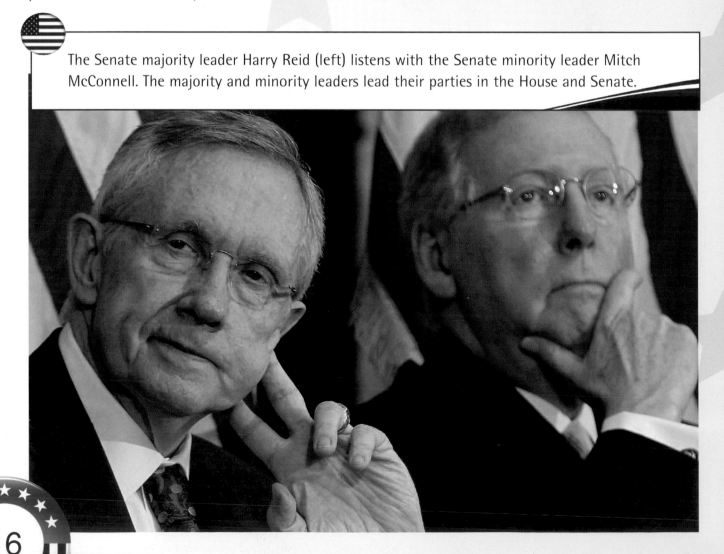

The Senate majority leader Harry Reid (left) listens with the Senate minority leader Mitch McConnell. The majority and minority leaders lead their parties in the House and Senate.

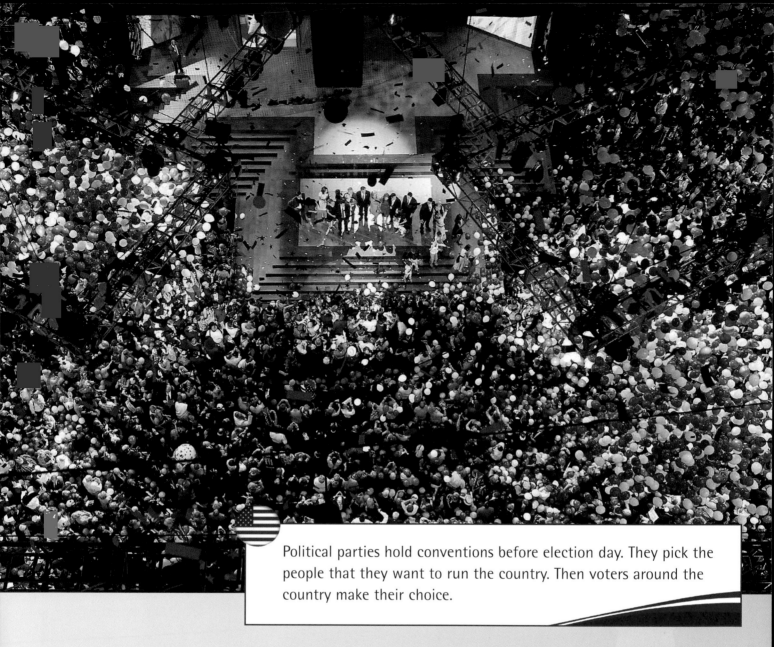

Political parties hold conventions before election day. They pick the people that they want to run the country. Then voters around the country make their choice.

The majority party has more power. If all its members vote the same way, it has the most votes. Members of the majority party pick leaders in both the House and Senate to speak on their behalf.

The minority party also picks leaders in both the House and Senate. The minority party often works against the majority. It sometimes tries to block the bills that the majority party tries to pass.

WHAT DO YOU THINK?

How many seats must a party hold to have a majority in the Senate? How many seats in the House?

Why Two Houses?

Why do House representatives and senators sit in two different houses? Why are they elected for different terms?

The House and the Senate look at laws in different ways. Each has different duties. The short term of the representatives means many members are new and eager. The senators serve longer terms and have more experience.

These differences help the two houses balance each other. The House of Representatives treats all Americans equally. The Senate treats every state equally. This way, big states do not have more power than smaller ones.

Each year, the president speaks to both the House and the Senate at the same time during the State of the Union address.

Once bills are passed by the House and the Senate, the president signs them into law.

These differences mean that the House and the Senate sometimes disagree. Bills cannot become law if the two do not work together. The two houses sometimes have to **negotiate** with each other to get work done.

In Their Own Words

"The Congress shall assemble at least once in every Year . . ."
The U.S. **Constitution**, Article I

The Whips

Majority parties often can only pass their bills if all of their members vote the same way. Minority parties are only powerful when their members agree with each other. To make sure this happens, both parties have whips.

These are not real whips, but powerful people. They make sure the lawmakers vote with the party on bills. Sometimes lawmakers do not vote the way the whips tell them to. If this happens, they can be punished. Sometimes the lawmakers lose their power in the party or they can even be kicked out of the party.

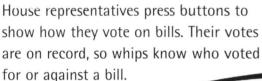

House representatives press buttons to show how they vote on bills. Their votes are on record, so whips know who voted for or against a bill.

Representatives sometimes have to choose between their voters and their party.

House or Senate members sometimes disagree with their party's position on a bill. A bill might not be good for the lawmaker's district. The lawmaker's decision to vote yes or no can be very difficult.

WHAT DO YOU THINK?

Why is it important that members of a party vote the same way?

Debating and Voting

Lawmakers make laws by introducing bills to the floor of the House or the Senate. Lawmakers spend a lot of time talking about their bills. They tell other lawmakers why each bill should or should not be passed. This is called a **debate**.

The House and the Senate have their own rules about how long lawmakers can talk about a bill. The House—having more members—keeps talking time short.

A majority of representatives can vote to stop talking and start voting. In the Senate, 60 senators have to vote to stop a debate from happening.

Bills that pass through one house must go to the other. They face the same process. Once approved, the bill is sent to the president. He or she must sign it to make it a law.

Making a bill into law takes a lot of talking and a lot of paperwork.

Senator Bernie Sanders spoke for eight hours straight for his filibuster against a Senate bill. The longest filibuster was 24 hours, 18 minutes.

One senator can affect the vote with a **filibuster**. A filibuster is when a senator or a group of senators can talk about a bill for as long as they choose. This delays the voting on a bill. To end the filibuster, 60 out of the 100 senators must vote to stop it. Otherwise, the filibuster goes on.

Committee Hearings

Once a lawmaker proposes a bill, it usually goes to a committee. These committees are made up of lawmakers from the minority and majority parties. The majority party always holds the most votes on a committee.

In a committee, people look at how the bill should be worded. Lawmakers bring in experts to speak about the bill. They talk about the impact of the bill and whether it will be good for the country.

House and Senate committees meet in special rooms in the Capitol.

Before she joined the Supreme Court, Judge Sonia Sotomayor had to appear before a committee.

Committee hearings are treated like a court of law. Witnesses must promise to tell the truth. Sometimes witnesses do not show up, or they lie. As punishment, they can be fined up to $1,000 or put in jail for up to one year.

Committees suggest changes to bills. They decide whether it can go back to the House or the Senate for a vote. Sometimes bills "die in committee."

This happens when committees take too long to look at a bill. The bill then has to be presented again to Congress.

WHAT DO YOU THINK?

How does the majority party control committees?

The President's Veto

Once a bill passes both houses, the president must sign it into law. But the president can **veto** a bill. *Veto* is Latin for "I forbid." Sometimes the president believes the bill is badly written. Or, the president may disagree with Congress on what bills are good for the country.

A vetoed bill goes back to Congress. To defeat the veto, the House and Senate must pass the bill again. This time, two-thirds of all representatives and senators must support the bill.

President Obama vetoed two bills in his first term in office. There was not support from two-thirds of Congress, so the bills could not be passed again.

Representatives are elected every two years. The president is elected every four years. Senators are elected every six years. Because of this, the relationship of the House, the Senate, and the president can change. This can lead to arguments as the two houses and the president all try to run the country.

President Franklin D. Roosevelt vetoed more than 600 bills. That was more vetoes than any other president. He was elected to office four times.

Blocking Bills

Sometimes the value of stocks on Wall Street fall when Congress and the president do not work together.

Sometimes Congress and the president disagree. An argument can affect the whole country. Congress passes bills, but the president signs them into law. If the two do not work together, bills do not get passed. Laws do not get made and government work can stop.

There are limits to what the government can do. It cannot keep spending without a budget. A budget is a plan for how money will be earned and spent. Without a bill that allows spending, many government services would shut down.

In Their Own Words

"Congress shall have Power To . . . collect Taxes . . . to pay the Debts and provide for the common Defence and general Welfare of the United States."
The U.S. Constitution, Article I

Sometimes the people have to take action themselves to get things done. In 1963, more than 200,000 people marched in Washington, D.C. They wanted Congress to pass laws protecting equal rights for all Americans

In 1995 and 1996, Congress and President Bill Clinton argued over how the government should be run. They could not pass a budget. The government shut down. Every part of the United States was affected. Government workers were not paid. National parks and museums closed.

These arguments can end when both sides talk to each other. In order to reach an agreement, sometimes a compromise needs to happen. This is where they each give up part of their demands so the outcome is acceptable to both sides.

Other Governments

The U.S. government is like governments in other countries. The House of Representatives is like the British House of Commons. Both are elected by people in districts, and both make laws.

The Senate is like the British House of Lords. Both vote on bills passed to them by the House. The president is like the queen or king of Great Britain. Both sign bills into law.

The president has more power than the queen of Great Britain.

Canada has a House of Commons and a Senate. The 301 members of the House of Commons are elected. The Senate has 105 members. Like the United States, Australia has a House of Representatives and a Senate. All members are elected.

The U.S. government looks at laws carefully before they affect Americans. This can lead to delays or fights. But it is better than having no elected officials at all. The American people need to make sure the best people are elected to Congress. Proper elections make sure that lawmakers make the best laws to serve their country.

Most people age 18 and older can and should vote.

DISCUSSION QUESTIONS

1. Lawmakers vote on bills that affect many people in both their district and the entire country. Discuss the different factors that can influence a lawmaker's vote.

2. Many people around the world feel the right to vote is one of the most important rights a person can have. Why do you think it is important for citizens to be able to vote?

Learning More

Books

Bright-Moore, Susan. *How Is a Law Passed?* Crabtree Publishing, 2008.

Giddens-White, Bryon. *Congress and the Legislative Branch*. Heinemann Library, 2006.

Websites

Kids in the House:
kids.clerk.house.gov/grade-school

Government for Kids:
www.ducksters.com/history/us_legislative_branch.php

Glossary

Congress The United States' legislative body of elected members that consist of both the House of Representatives and the Senate

Constitution A paper telling how the U.S. government is to be run

debate An argument about a topic

district An area of the country

filibuster When a senator tries to block a vote on a bill by talking for a long period of time

majority Describes the group with more than half of the votes

minority Describes the group with fewer than half of the votes

negotiate To talk and make deals so that something you want happens

political party A group of people that share the same views on how a country should be run

preside To supervise, manage, or control

representatives Individuals who speak for other people when those people cannot speak for themselves

staggered Arranged so things happen at different times

veto To reject a choice made by others

Index